HAL•LEONARD
Classical
PLAY-ALONG™

Volume 9

Joseph
HAYDN
(1732-1809)

Cello Concerto in C Major, Hob. VIIb: 1

The Hal Leonard Classical Play-Along™ series allows you to work through great classical works systematically and at any tempo with accompaniment.

Tracks 2-3 on the CD demonstrate the concert version of each movement. After tuning your instrument to Track 1 you can begin practicing the piece. Using the Amazing Slow-Downer technology included on the CD, you can adjust the recording to any tempo you like without altering the pitch. (Note that when using Amazing Slow-Downer, the CD will stop after each track instead of playing continuously.) The full cadenzas are played only in the concert version.

- Track No. ☐1 – tuning notes
- Track numbers in circles ◯ – concert version
- Track numbers in diamonds ◆ – play-along version

CONCERT VERSION

Kyrill Rodin, Cello

Russian Philharmonic Orchestra Moscow

Konstantin Krimets, Conductor

ISBN 978-1-4234-6248-4

HAL•LEONARD®
CORPORATION
7777 W. BLUEMOUND RD. P.O. BOX 13819 MILWAUKEE, WI 53213

In Australia Contact:
Hal Leonard Australia Pty. Ltd.
4 Lentara Court
Cheltenham, Victoria, 3192 Australia
Email: ausadmin@halleonard.com.au

Visit Hal Leonard Online at
www.halleonard.com

CONCERTO Hob. VIIb:1

for Cello in C Major

I ②

J. Haydn (1732-1809)

7

II ③